What others are saying about
YOUR PARTNER HAS BREAST CANCER:

"Ken has in a thoughtful and caring way shared effective ways that worked for him as he was a great husband and father supporting his wife and children in his family's battle against breast cancer. I am confident that these ways will have a powerful impact in helping all support people, but especially guys who may be struggling, to be loving partners as they battle breast cancer in their families."
—Marc Heyison, President/Founder, Men Against Breast Cancer www.menagainstbreastcancer.org

"All I can say is wow! I found this book helpful, informative, moving, and clearly a labor of love."
—Dr. Helen Pass, Director, Division of Breast Surgery, and Co-Director of Women's Breast Center, Stamford Hospital, Stamford, CT

"The story is masterfully told, the advice lovingly conveyed…. [a] tremendous help to people whose lives have been turned upside down, especially support people, whose journeys through diagnosis and treatment of cancer can be lonely and confusing."
—Cantor Ann Zibelman Rose, Facilitator of Temple Beth Emeth Caring Community, Ann Arbor, Michigan

"… should give every caregiver hope"
—Diana Dyer, MS, RD, author of A Dietician's Cancer Story www.cancerrd.com

"Ken's book is a much-needed and welcome addition to the cancer literature. His advice is simple, clear, and compassionate."
—*Eileen Coan, Medical Librarian, The Gathering Place www.touchedbycancer.org, Beachwood, Ohio*

"Recommended for public libraries and especially for libraries with strong consumer health collections."
—*Sarah Watstein, Director, Academic User Services, Virginia Commonwealth University*

" WOWIE WOW WOW! As a human being who has gone through my own medical challenges, I loved it. I found the advice to be very sound and very helpful. Your personal story really engages me in a deep way.... And I connect with you so easily and on a very personal level."
—*Kristi Davis, Founder, Creative Spirit Healing*

YOUR PARTNER HAS BREAST CANCER
2nd edition

21 Ways to Keep Sane as a Support Person on Your Journey from Victim to Survivor

Ken Wachsberger

Azenphony Press
Ann Arbor, MI

Published by
Azenphony Press
PO Box 130884
Ann Arbor, MI 48113-0884
U.S.A.
info@azenphonypress.com
www.azenphonypess.com
734-635-0577

Your Partner Has Breast Cancer, 2nd edition
Copyright May 12, 2014 by Ken Wachsberger
ISBN 978-0-945531-10-4 (pbk)
ISBN 978-0-945531-05-0 (ebook)

Cover and formatting by caligraphics.net
Back cover photo by Carrie Wachsberger

All rights reserved.
No parts of this book may be reproduced in any
form without written permission from the publisher.

DEDICATION

The perceived breast cancer victim is the person who goes into surgery, and with good reason. But the support person, the caregiver, is the silent victim, the one who takes over the perceived victim's chores, answers questions for well-wishers, assumes double-income responsibility and becomes both parents if they are in a formal couple relationship, and is always the pillar of strength, even when he or she doesn't feel like a pillar of strength.

This book is dedicated to the silent victims—especially husbands, who form by far the largest bloc of support persons and yet are the most inept at asking for help. I know because I was one of them. When I needed help for myself, I found a lot of material on how I could help my spouse but nothing on how I could help myself while I was helping her. This book is what I needed then; I am confident it is exactly what you need now.

You can't help your partner if you aren't helping yourself.

But, my sisters, it is you who likely will have to invest in this book (as if you have nothing else to think about) because your partner is probably denying he needs the help. It's a smooth read, it's uplifting, and the steps are easy to implement. Help him to help you.

Join me on the path from victim to survivor.

ACKNOWLEDGMENTS

Thanks from Emily, David, Carrie, and me to everyone in our support network who were there when we needed you, even when we didn't know we needed you, including family and friends; doctors, nurses, social workers, and staff at University of Michigan Hospital's Breast Cancer Division; and Rabbi Bob Levy, Cantor Annie Rose, and the Caring Community at Temple Beth Emeth.

Thanks to Emily, David, and Carrie for keeping me honest and strong, as always

YOUR PARTNER HAS BREAST CANCER
2nd edition
21 Ways to Keep Sane as a Support Person on Your Journey from Victim to Survivor

TABLE OF CONTENTS

DEDICATION	v
ACKNOWLEDGMENTS	vii
A WORD FROM THE AUTHOR	xi
PANIC IS STEP ONE. TIME FOR STEP TWO	1
SOME MOTHER'S DAY THIS IS!	2
21 WAYS TO KEEP SANE AS A SUPPORT PERSON	9
1. Keep a journal	9
2. Be the family reporter	10
3. Share your feelings and thoughts with your partner as much as possible	12
4. Let it out every now and then	15
5. Have at least one confidante besides your partner	16
6. Be honest with your children and get them involved in their mother's recovery	17
7. Laugh whenever you can	19
8. Accept help from anyone who offers	20
9. Read the literature	22
10. Participate in your partner's recovery	24

11. At the same time, don't succumb to guilt	25
12. Don't feel the need to "fix" things	26
13. Find a spiritual comfort zone you can share	27
14. Eat well	28
15. Exercise regularly	29
16. Sleep enough	30
17. Take a deep breath often	31
18. Find time to be alone when you need alone time	32
19. At the same time, get used to being alone when you want company	33
20. Nurture your creative outlets whatever they are	34
21. And be patient	35
THE CANCER JOURNALS	37
RESOURCES FOR CAREGIVERS	77
FINAL WORD TO READERS	83
OTHER BOOKS BY KEN WACHSBERGER	85
ABOUT THE AUTHOR	87

A WORD FROM THE AUTHOR

This is the second edition of *Your Partner Has Breast Cancer*. It includes three new and important additions to enhance the first edition.

The first is "The Cancer Journals." Although I wrote the journals, they are more about Emily than about me. The first edition was published not long after Emily's final chemo treatment. The experience was still raw for her and what I wrote about still felt too close, so she requested that I not publish them and I honored her request.

Now it's fourteen years later. No one ever finishes having breast cancer. Although both of us consider ourselves survivors rather than victims, we still wake up every day thinking "I/my partner had breast cancer." We always will.

But Emily is in good health and far enough from the experience that she had no problem giving me permission. For that I'm thankful. Since the first way to keep sane that I describe in this book is to keep a journal and the second is to share it, my hope with this second edition is that support people will see it as a role model.

The second addition is a list of resources for caregivers. Fourteen years after I wrote the first edition, there still is a dearth of resources on how to take care of yourself while you're helping your partner. But it is a growing field. I have included a few samples.

Finally, I've added the phrase "on Your Journey from Victim to Survivor" to the subtitle to highlight my focus on our goal of becoming survivors, not remaining trapped as victims.

—Ken Wachsberger
Ann Arbor, Michigan

Panic is step one.
Time for step two.

You just found out that your partner has breast cancer.

You're feeling panic because you will be expected to be her main support partner during her recovery period and you don't think you can do it.

Good.

Panic is step one. It means you care.

But now it's time to move to step two, your action plan, so that when you arrive at step three, after the initial recovery period, you will be feeling closer to her and to yourself than you've ever felt in your life.

I did it. You can, too.

Some Mother's Day this is!

On May 12, the Friday before Mother's Day 2000, Emily's biopsy report came in. It was positive. Cancer cells had gone beyond the 9 mm tumor that the surgeon had removed from her left breast. How far? The report couldn't say.

Three days later, Monday, we spent all day at the cancer center of University of Michigan Hospital (UMH) giving blood, being x-rayed again, and reading the hospital's Web literature on breast cancer.

We wanted to know why the x-rays hadn't shown the cancer cells that lay outside the 9 mm lump. The surgeons didn't know. And now, although her right breast was shown to be clear, how could we know that it was really clear?

Emily's decision was quick and definitive—she wanted a double mastectomy with a complete reconstructive surgery that would use tissue stretched up from her abdomen, and she wanted to get it over with as soon as possible.
I supported her decision absolutely.

Two days later, we got the word that the hospital had assembled the two teams—general surgery and plastic surgery—for an operation two days later, the next Friday.

And so from Friday to Friday we got the bad news, learned the extent of the problem, made our decision, and had the complete 12 ½-hour surgery. Four days later, she came home to begin her long recuperation, still with drains hanging from four points in her body.

It was fortunate financially that I worked at home because I could be her primary care provider during the day. Because she couldn't bathe, dress, or get in and out of bed or her chair without help, I was constantly on call to help with those mundane tasks that we normally take for granted.

At night, I helped her empty the drains and measure fluid output. Because she couldn't drive or lift more than the weight of a soup can, I took up the shopping and cooking, normally on her end of the division of labor in our household. She couldn't bend easily so I took over care of the outside garden.

In addition, when friends and relatives called to find out what happened, I took the calls so Emily could rest. The responsibility for providing updates also was carried by me.

Meanwhile, I tried to be both parents to our son and daughter.

I fell way behind in my work and felt the enormous strain of impending deadlines. I felt guilt at being unable to assume my caretaker responsibilities with more ease. I denied the legitimacy of my feelings because Emily was the designated victim. I held out nobly.

Three weeks into Emily's recovery, a friend called to inquire about Emily's status. As I was performing my supporting role function of providing an update, my friend interrupted me to ask, "Ken, how are you feeling?"

Oh, yeah. I paused.

My first reaction was to stifle tears so I wouldn't choke on my answer. I used words like "surreal" and "fatigued." But I didn't refer to "panic," "freak out," or any other indication of desperation.

In fact, now that I thought about it, I was doing okay. What a relief, because hanging over my head always was the memory of a friend whose husband couldn't handle his supporting role during her cancer ordeal and left her. That negative role model was my inspiration to do better.

But what exactly did I do right? And how could I maintain my positive mental health over what was still destined to be a long recovery period?

To answer my questions, I sought advice from professionals and others who had gone through what I was still only beginning, considered it with an open mind, and picked and chose to fit my temperament. I looked for literature on the Web. At times I went with my gut feeling and was just lucky. I knew an end was in sight and that we would emerge victorious.

If your partner has breast cancer, there's a good chance you will emerge victorious, too.

Keep that in mind when you think your world is going to end prematurely.

Emily endured her fourth and final chemotherapy treatment as I was completing the first edition of this book. She is now in her fourteenth year of recovery. We hung together. I've never felt closer to her. You can, too (to your partner, not mine), if you follow these 21 ways to keep sane while supporting your partner through breast cancer.

The occurrence statistic that keeps popping up in my research shows only 1 in 100 perceived victims being male. Given, therefore, that 99% of perceived victims are female and the majority of couple relationships are heterosexual, the vast majority of silent victims are male.

So, my brothers in silent victimhood, because we need help the most and yet are socialized to not look inside ourselves or reach out to others, this book is dedicated to you. You can't help your partner if you aren't helping yourself.

But, my sisters, it is you who likely will have to invest in this book (as if you have nothing else to think about) because your partner is—actively or passively—denying he needs the help.

I know we guys can be pretty literal: I was a math major in an earlier life. So, my brothers, let me note here that I listed the 21 ways in the order that made the most sense to me but you can implement them in any order you want. In fact, if you want to skip some of them altogether and focus on others, that's okay, too.

One final note: The literature on breast cancer likes to refer to those of us who have been through the breast cancer adventure as survivors, not victims. I'm all for it. I'm a survivor.

But there is more to being a survivor than calling yourself one, although that is a necessary first step. If you just found out today that your mate has breast cancer, you feel like a victim, not a survivor, and so does she. If she just had her surgery yesterday, you feel like a victim, not a survivor, and so does she.

Be patient, be positive, take the actions described in this book, as many as you want to implement and in whatever order you choose, and you'll get there. You'll discover a whole new, wonderful community of folks like you who have been through it and are doing fine. And you'll discover a whole new, wonderful side of yourself and your partner.

Being a survivor is the vision. In this book, I begin where many of you are now. But I won't let you stay there.

21 ways to keep sane as a support person

1. Keep a journal

If you've ever wanted to "be a writer" when you grew up, you should be doing this anyhow.

But if you've never in your worst nightmare thought seriously about becoming a writer and to this day have no plans to become one, still you can write to stay grounded; you'll need a lot of that to get through this experience standing strong and proud.

If you don't know how to get started and don't know what to write about, begin by writing, "I don't know how to get started; I don't know what to write about," and write exactly whatever comes to your mind for the next 20 minutes.

Give yourself a special time every day. If you have an aversion to writing because you can't conjugate verbs or pluralize nouns, relax because no one has to see what you write but you.

2. Be the family reporter

That's a big role you've got to play anyhow but it becomes much easier once you begin keeping a journal. Here's one reason why: By the time you recover from the initial shock that cancer is in your family and you are beginning to regain equilibrium, a lot has happened, and everyone wants to know the chronological details.

Guess what.

During her early recovery period, with your partner sleeping more than usual and often drugged up in her waking hours, it becomes your job to let significant others—friends; family; colleagues and fellow workers, yours and hers; the guy you never knew until you both discovered that you shared supporting role status in the same condition—know "What happened, what's happening, and what's next?"

Get it down once and send an email burst to everyone you want to know or you figure will be calling you anyhow to inquire. Then provide periodic updates. You anticipate their Level 1 questions and answer them along with some of their Level 2 questions.

When they call you, it's to offer the emotional support you need, not to grill you with the same questions everyone else has been asking.

And sharing your experience helps your loved ones past a peculiar human hang-up. At the exact time when you and your partner are most in need of all-out, no-holds-barred love—in the form of prayers, blessings, flowers, cards, meals, and other unbridled shows of emotional and physical support—many of your loved ones will deliberately withhold it because they think that acknowledging your condition to you will remind you of it and make you feel bad.

As if there is ever a moment when you're not thinking about it anyhow.

Writing to them first tells them that it's okay for them to talk about it with you. You give them permission to give you support.

3. Share your feelings and thoughts with your partner as much as possible

There's a thin line between being strong, which is good, and being unfeeling, which is bad. And sometimes timing is everything.

When Emily learned that she had breast cancer, she was at work. Stunned, she called me to share the bad news. I told her I would bring her home.

On my way to pick her up, I thought about what I had just learned and I imagined possible outcomes. I was alternately terrified and calm. I wondered how I should react when I saw her. Should I be strong and show no fear so that she could see I was her protector? Or should I break down sobbing in her arms because I was scared of losing her? I rationalized that I had to keep my cool because I had to drive us home.

As I pulled into the parking lot, Kathie, our friend, who had been waiting in the lobby, came out to meet me. She climbed into the front seat and asked right away, "How are you feeling?"

Her question surprised me; I was waiting to hear how Emily was doing. I started to cry softly, not difficult if I didn't say a lot.

I answered Kathie's question in sentence fragments. But I dutifully kept my cool. "Are you ready to go in?" Kathie asked. I held back my tears, wiped my eyes, and nodded that I was ready.

Emily was by now deep in shock; when she saw me she began crying again. I let myself cry in our embrace but forced myself to remain composed.

Later that evening, while Emily was asleep, I sat downstairs at my computer and cried freely. At the time, it was the right decision.

Six weeks later, by now 12 days after Emily's first chemotherapy treatment, I lost my job. Emily was physically and emotionally fragile. In addition, she's the one in our partnership who traditionally has handled the bill paying so when money is tight she's the first to feel the stress.

I didn't tell her for three weeks because I didn't want to add to her stress. In retrospect, I'm glad I waited as I did. But holding on to that secret did little to enhance my own emotional well-being.

Only after a trip together to our nutritional oncologist, where I witnessed a new level of strength and confidence on Emily's part, was I willing to take a chance and tell her. I steeled myself to the possibility that she would panic that we were going to lose the house, and I prepared to condemn myself for hindering her progress by being so self-centered.

To my surprise, she was calm, confident, resigned, spiritual. "The worst that'll happen is we lose the house, we move to an apartment, and I support us on my salary," she said, adding, "All that matters is that I'm alive."

Once she knew, I could begin to work out a job-hunting strategy with her in the support role. The role reversal was empowering to us both.

If such open communication is more than you've ever been able to handle by yourself, know that a support network already is in place in your hospital and community. Social workers, psychiatrists, support groups, religious leaders, interested individuals, and, of course, your surgeons and their assistants are there for you. Visit them with your partner.

They may not know you need help until you ask for it.

So ask for it.

4. Let it out every now and then

If you're the macho man who grew up thinking it was cowardly to cry, then do it in private in front of a mirror until you're comfortable seeing your eyes with tears in them.

If you're already the sensitive male who isn't afraid to show your emotions, you're far into this experience already.

Now try sharing those feelings with your partner, a little at a time, and see how she reacts. Always be going in the direction of sharing and do so always at your first opportunity.

Remember that breast cancer is a culture of wellness, not of sickness. Our nurse told us this. So did our surgeon. Once the cancer cells are removed, the healing begins. As I described in the examples above, look for signs of new strength and added insight in your partner. These are opportunities for you to move your relationship to a higher level.

5. Have at least one confidante besides your partner

The mantra during breast cancer surgery and recovery for progressive cancer hospitals like University of Michigan Hospital is "Control the pain."

Your partner will be given drugs to control pain, drugs to control nausea, drugs to control anxiety. And they will.

But she'll be tired and spaced out a lot while they're performing their tasks. The first four days after each chemotherapy treatment, for instance, are considered the worst so your partner may be given special drugs to take just on those days.

If you need intimacy during that period, forget it. She's somewhere else.

Suggestion: Your email blasts go to everybody at once. You can develop individual relationships with the ones who respond, and many do. Answer their answers, even if just to say, "Thanks for thinking of us." You find confidantes often in this group.

6. Be honest with your children and get them involved in their mother's recovery

Put another way, do you think there's any way you will be able to hide from their perceptive eyes the fact that something's wrong?

Here's the bad news: Breast cancer is an epidemic. Tell anyone you're fighting breast cancer and you are sure to hear, "Oh, yeah, my wife had breast cancer/my mother had breast cancer/my sister had breast cancer."

But here's the good news: Children today have a different connotation of breast cancer than did those of us who grew up in the fifties and sixties and seventies. Then, breast cancer was more likely a death sentence. Today, women are surviving it. Your children can handle the news.

We've always educated David and Carrie about the importance of family. Sometimes, probably usually, our "education" has come across as parents harping to get their kids to stop arguing with each other.

But that first Friday, May 12, we had our first of four family breast cancer meetings to share with them what we knew (the other three: the following Monday after we made the decision to go for a double mastectomy with complete reconstructive surgery; two days later to announce that the surgery was set for that Friday; and the next week when the report came in that Emily's lymph nodes were clear).

We explained that this was an example of the importance of family that we always talked about. We let them know that we were scared and that it was okay. But we also let them know that we were facing the future with confidence.

We asked them if they had any questions and I don't recall that they did. But in order to draw out their feelings, we asked yes/no questions, in particular, "Are you scared?"

They were, "a little." And that was okay. Carrie noted to Emily, "Your mother had breast cancer and she's okay. Her sister had breast cancer and she's okay. You'll be okay."

In the days to follow, they continued to do their usual chores, but they did more as well: 11-year old Carrie cooked some dinners; 17-year old David allowed himself to be on call with the car to run errands. And I'm sure they argued less with each other.

7. Laugh whenever you can

We've always tried to do things as a family. Family dinner. Family vacation. Family hug.

Okay, Emily got carried away that one time when she suggested a family floss after dinner, but you get the point.

After our first family meeting, we were all emotionally drained. Emily called for a family hug. We embraced.

David, who already towered over all of us, caught a mouthful of Emily's hair and went "pttt" to spit it out. Laughter broke the tension but David was embarrassed until I thanked him for reminding us that we needed to laugh now more than ever.

8. Accept help from anyone who offers

When friends offered to help, I didn't know what to tell them to do.

But when Martha and Mary brought meals the first week, and when Kathie washed Emily's hair and Lorraine gave her a hand shower before she was able to wash herself, I was able to spend those extra hours working on the computer catching up from the work time I had lost since Mother's Day weekend.

The second week, Bev brought a Middle Eastern spread of tabouli, hummus, baba gannoujj, rice, pita, peppers, and salad on Monday. Tuesday, Judith brought pasta and salad. Wednesday, we ate leftovers.

Although we aren't overly observant in our religious traditions, we found comfort from visits by our rabbi and our cantor. On more than one occasion, they joined us in meditation.

After the first week of recovery, we had round-the-clock help from a synchronized network of friends and relatives that included my parents, Emily's mother, a niece, a sister-in-law, Carrie's godmother, and David's godmother.

By the time the last link of that support chain packed up and returned home, Emily was driving again and even able to lift some grocery bags.

I felt some pressure during that time to be the perfect partner and I was pulled toward wanting to be there for Emily's every need. But I was so overwhelmed by the outpouring of love and support, not to mention my own shock and denial, that I gave up and accepted all help without judging.

The Force was with me on that decision even when I was forgetting that I was a victim, too.

9. Read the literature

There's a lot of literature out there on breast cancer (though not much on how to stay sane as a support person; hence, this book), and it's everywhere: at the hospital, the acupuncturist's office, the nutritional oncologist's office, any of the many cancer societies, the library.

In researching how to stay sane as a support person, I didn't use the Web at all until well into Emily's recovery because I didn't have the luxury of time to do online research. By the time I found some useful online sites and read their literature, it wasn't really useful to me.

But if you have use of a computer (and you do if you own a library card), search for the keyword combinations "cancer and spouse support" and "cancer and caregiver stress" and see what you find.

Make sure you visit Empowering Caregivers and Men Against Breast Cancer.

According to their own background data, Empowering Caregivers was founded in October 1998 on AOL by Gail Mitchell, presumably to help herself in her own recovery, although the website doesn't answer that question. Two weeks later, they published their first newsletter online. In December, the site was launched.

Besides offering their newsletter for free twice weekly, the site has recommended books, links to online and offline sources, a directory of alternative healing sources, humor, and more. The weekly chats are reason enough to log on if you don't have a confidante with whom you can share thoughts and ideas when your partner is unavailable.

Men Against Breast Cancer was founded by Marc Heyison in 1999, the first and only national 501 (c)(3) nonprofit organization designed to provide targeted support services that educate and empower men to be effective cancer caregivers. A particularly valuable feature is Find a Friend, an online resource for support people looking for other support people in their community to share thoughts and feelings. It also includes a collection of websites with useful breast cancer- and cancer-in-general-related information; non-web information sources about breast cancer; and video resources.

10. Participate in your partner's recovery

Being conversant in the literature of breast cancer is an important first step in your becoming a supportive player in your partner's recovery.

But support doesn't stop with the intellectual understanding. You've got to get involved as much as possible.

As we learned, there is "curing" and there is "healing." Curing involves getting rid of the physical symptoms, the cancer cells; healing involves repairing the malfunctions of our own internal system: our lifestyle, our attitudes, our diet, the disconnect between our dreams and our reality, and, yes, our personal relationships.

No, you aren't the cause of your partner's cancer. But you are a vital part of her healing process. Become immersed in the culture and the recovery; she already is.

When your partner has cancer, you have cancer. Her recovery is your recovery. Go with her as much as possible to the treatments and sessions that are part of her healing process.

11. At the same time, don't succumb to guilt

It's a balancing act. You'll stumble. Just keep getting up.

During Cancer Survivors' Day in Washtenaw County, I was with Emily at the celebration. Even when she was driving again, I went with her to her chemotherapy treatments, her acupuncture sessions, her visits to our nutritional oncologist, and her plastic surgeon, and we continued to meditate together twice a week.

But I let her go alone, once she was driving, to her physical therapist, her chiropractor, and her physical massages.

I couldn't do it all so I drew the line and stepped to one side.

12. Don't feel the need to "fix" things

I learned that lesson the hard way.

Around the time of her second chemotherapy treatment, Emily's hair began falling out. Then it became noticeable.

She started to cry while we were taking a walk when someone looked at her and she was convinced he thought she was hideous. To me, she still looked beautiful but I know I would be self-conscious, too, if it were me whose hair was falling out.

I told her that he was probably admiring how brave she was or some such stupid comment that was exactly the wrong reply to make at that time.

She rebuked my effort to make her feel better and let me know that she was strong 90% of the time but that sometimes she had to feel the sadness.

I let her feel her sadness then and didn't say anything else until she asked me to continue what I had been saying before the interruption.

13. Find a spiritual comfort zone you can share

For Emily and me, it was meditating and learning about the Kabbalah, the book of Jewish mysticism.

Individually, we meditated wherever and whenever we chose. Emily favored the backyard in the afternoon; my place and time of choice were in bed upon waking and before going to sleep. Together, we meditated two times a week at the chapel in our Temple.

The morning of her first chemotherapy treatment, we stopped in for a session. In my chair, I slouched, I sat straight, I sat with hands clasped on my lap trying to find a comfortable position to hold for 20 minutes. I sat with my hands hanging to the side and with my hands resting one on each lap and all the while I meditated, sometimes aware of my squirming, at others not.

While I was meditating, I saw the Joy in this greater occasion and concluded, without understanding exactly why, that my vision was logical. When I told Emily what I had seen, she said she had seen three words: Love, Kindness, and Strength.

I asked her to add Joy, and then to consider with me those four words as our mantra.

14. Eat well

I know. I just said I saw Joy while I was meditating. That became part of our vision, but it wasn't always part of my reality. Having a partner with breast cancer can feel pretty lousy. Life is treating you like a throw rug. What better time to pity yourself and pig out on junk food? Can it make you feel worse than you're already feeling?

Well, yes. And it will.

So watch what you eat. This may not be the time to begin researching how to eat organically, or how to prepare a diet in line with your blood type. You've got other concerns. What is important is to not sacrifice your current diet to your grief.

If you're already thinking that your eating habits are unhealthy and in need of upgrading, plan to visit your local nutritionist when you're ready to make a change. For now, the point is to not relax your current dietary habits because you don't have time. Make the time. You need your strength because your spouse doesn't have hers.

15. Exercise regularly

You don't have to join a fitness club because your wife has breast cancer. This isn't the time to start training for your first marathon. But you do need to keep your body in shape so you can help your partner take care of hers. If your life is currently devoid of physical exertion, start slowly.

Stretching is one of the most invigorating forms of exercise I know, as well as a major stress reliever. I have a regular routine that starts at my neck and goes down to my feet. But stretching isn't enough. You need to do some cardio exercises as well to get your heart pumping.

Take a walk around the block. The next day do the same but increase your pace until you're walking briskly. Don't just put one foot in front of the other. Stretch while you walk, and increase your stride so you can feel your muscles. What a great opportunity to visit the parks in your community.

Suggestion: Find a friend to share in your exercising, not only for the encouragement your friend will give you to keep moving but for the company you crave when you're feeling lonely.

16. Sleep enough

The recommended sleep time is eight hours a night but I would be hypocritical if I told you to stick to that regimen. I only sleep six hours myself on an average weekend night, less during the week.

But I've been known to fall asleep on the couch while watching TV.

Bottom line: If you're tired during the day, you need more sleep. It doesn't have to all be at once. An hour in the middle of the day—even 15 minutes—does wonders for the rest of the day.

17. Take a deep breath often

Are you eating well? Are you exercising regularly? Are you sleeping enough?
You won't know if you keep plowing ahead in the name of "helping your partner."

So stop every now and then. That's it—just stop.

And take a deep breath. In through the nose, expanding first your stomach, then your chest, to take in as much air as possible. Hold.
Then out through the mouth, slowly collapsing first your chest and then your stomach. Hold.
Repeat.

There is no better way to relieve stress than with a series of slow, deep breaths. Even one is helpful, but give yourself a gift and do sets of five throughout the day, whenever you think about it. Treat yourself like the good person that you are.

At the same time, you can listen to your body and do what it is telling you to do.

18. Find time to be alone when you need alone time

Remember that journal you started keeping so you could be the family reporter? You need alone time to do it.

But even when you aren't writing, you need time just to reflect on what's going on.

Sometimes it's pretty dramatic—like the days when she gets her chemo doses. Other times, it's almost mundane, just another day.

You also need time to get back in touch with yourself, to forget about what's going on and let your mind wander to where it wants to go.

How long? At minimum, time enough to take those deep breaths, but really you can do better than that. Wait until she's sleeping and doesn't need your active attention, or find a time when someone from your support network is watching her. You can drive her to her doctor's appointment and then let her go in alone while you take a walk or wait for her at the nearby coffee shop.

Every strong loving relationship has three partners: the You, the Me, and the Us. Nurture the Me so that you can be there for the You and the Us.

19. At the same time, get used to being alone when you want company

Even the best of confidantes aren't available 24x7. During those times when your partner is drugged up, asleep, or with one of her doctors and your confidantes are all living their own lives, you're out of luck if you're craving company.

On the positive side, hanging out with yourself has its own rewards. Take yourself to a movie. Read a book. Exercise.

Or …

20. Nurture your creative outlets whatever they are

Remember that book you always wanted to write? That room you always wanted to remodel? That instrument you always wanted to learn how to play? Don't let your newfound status as a support person be an excuse to let your own dream drift away. In fact, use it as a time to start living your dream.

Progress in the arts and trades doesn't come from six months straight of not doing anything but "creating." It comes from five minutes here, an hour there, maybe every now and then having a complete free day, but more often than not just grabbing bits and pieces of the day scattered throughout your regular tasks and habits.

Or taking advantage of those times when you would rather be with her but she just isn't there. Seek out those opportunities. Cherish them. Take advantage of them.

21. And be patient

Your breast cancer adventure is just a glitch in the road. As Emily kept reminding me, "This, too, shall pass."

And so shall your victimhood. In fact, it already has. By reading this book and beginning to follow the steps in the order of your choice, you have begun to take control of your new life situation. Congratulations. You're now a survivor.

Welcome to the first day of the rest of your life.

The Cancer Journals

The following passages were written partly as email bursts to family members and partly as personal journals.

When I published the first edition of this book in 2000, Emily was still too close to the experience and requested that I not include them. I'm grateful that she has now given me her okay.

I'd like to dedicate them to the memory of Lenore Bernstein, our friend and Emily's mentor during this adventure, who passed away on January 30, 2010. Lenore, her husband and our friend Jesse, and their children were sources of strength to us when we needed it.

Tuesday May 16, 2000

Hello, Pollack and Wachsberger Clans,

I'm writing to share some sad news. Emily was diagnosed with breast cancer Friday. Yesterday we spent the day at the hospital being tested and prodded. The doctors are all confident of a full recovery but it will include a bilateral mastectomy (for prophylactic reasons). We're waiting for word of a date, hopefully as soon as possible. She'll have the complete reconstruction done at the same time so she's looking at a 3-hour operation followed immediately by a 9-hour operation, then 10 weeks of recuperation and 24 weeks of chemo.

Yesterday was the saddest day of my life. I pray to God none of you have to go through it if you haven't already. Emily's a lot braver than I am. Her attitude is, she fed two beautiful kids with her breasts so she doesn't need them anymore, but, of course, she knows that's a rationalization. She couldn't sleep at all over the long weekend, Mother's Day, without popping two Xanaxes a night. Last night, after facing the long unknown without answers and finally receiving answers—not all good but at least answers—she was able to sleep with only one.

We've always educated David and Carrie about the importance of family. Sometimes, arguably usually, our "education" has come across as parents harping to get their kids to stop arguing with each other.

But Friday we had a family meeting and shared with them what we knew. We explained that this was an example of the importance of family that we always talked about. They understood and they were there with us so we could give each other support.

At the time, we "knew" that the cancer had gone to the walls of the section that had been taken out for the biopsy, which meant there was an unknown quantity of cancer still in her left breast. The x-ray showed a growth of 9 mm, less than a half inch, so we were confident. Emily's mother and her mother's sister both had growths removed also and they're healthy now. We gave the kids time to ask questions and express whatever feelings they had. Carrie senses it was no big deal since her grandmother and great aunt had survived the same operation. We were glad she felt that way. We ended with one of our traditional family hugs. We even were able to get in a laugh as David, who towers over all of us now, got some of Emily's hair in his mouth and spit it out. You can't ever forget the power of laughter.

At the hospital on Monday we learned that the x-ray hadn't picked up all the cancer growth. Stray cells had appeared beyond the growth of the tumor, which is not atypical of invasive ductile breast cancer, but which put Emily near the Stage 2 category. Why hadn't they noticed that before? They didn't know. Our fear became, what if there's cancer in the "healthy" right breast that they also aren't picking up? Emily faced the prospect of living the rest of her life in total paranoia. Her decision at that point was made for her.

We also, of course, wondered if the lymph nodes under her left arm had been attacked, and, if so, how spread out throughout the rest of the body the cancer cells had gone. The lungs perhaps?

Fortunately, Ann Arbor, with University of Michigan Hospital, may be the best place in the world to be if you're going to get cancer. At 1 p.m. everyday all the cancer surgeons meet to discuss all the patients who have undergone testing that morning. Then they begin their rounds talking to individual patients. We knew that if the lungs had been infested all talk of possible reconstruction would be moot, so when the oncologist, who will be seeing Emily every three weeks during the chemo stage, started talking about reconstruction and referring to Emily's cancer as a "garden-variety" type, meaning the kind they treat successfully every day, we both started crying, partly from exhaustion after the long weekend of not knowing.

Nevertheless, that doesn't mean that cancer cells HAVEN'T gotten into the lymph nodes. Most of those that do, the surgeon later explained, will be defeated by the body's natural immunity system. But, of course, some may make it. That's why the chemo is a standard part of UMH's treatment.

This oncologist, by the way, was a specialist in Ashkenazic Jews, who, if you don't know you probably should, have a genetic predisposition to breast cancer (not big, about 1%, but that's apparently higher than any other group, none of which, to my knowledge, are known to be "predisposed").

Before we left, the last surgeon gave Emily a prescription for a "cranial prosthesis." Do you know what that is? It's a wig (because Emily will lose her hair while she's having the chemo). But if they call it a wig the insurance won't pay for it. Next week, Emily is going cranial prosthesis shopping with our hair dresser.

Today Emily stayed home from work just to get some needed rest. We spent some time in the chapel at the Temple meditating with our chazzan, our cantor, who some of you might remember from David's Bar Mitzvah. It was interesting to learn that the Jewish meditation chant is Shalom, so close to the Eastern chant of Om that you wonder which came first and how closely related they might have been back when history was just starting to be written.

Anyhow, that's the update. Thanks for listening to me. Writing about it is my own best meditation.
By the way, we learned a danger of our New Age way of thinking. We've always believed that when you want something you have to put it out to the universe. Sometimes you get what you want but in ways that are unexpected: 1. Emily has wanted a tummy tuck for years. Now she's getting one, as part of her reconstructive surgery; 2. As someone who works

alone out of my home, I've regretted that Emily can't be here more often with me. Now she'll be here for at least six weeks after her surgery.

Love,
Ken

Wednesday May 24, 2000

Emily came home yesterday, ending the scariest 12 days of my life. A long recovery period is ahead but doctors are confident of a complete recovery. Emily's positive attitude will enhance her recovery.

Everything happened so fast, we barely had time to think, let alone change direction once we were set in motion. As I told you in my last letter, on Friday May12 we got the word that Emily had cancer.

What we did first was most important. We felt fear and didn't hide it. At our first meeting with David and Carrie, we let them know we were scared and that it was okay. But in line with our second move, we also let them know that we were facing the future with confidence.

Our second move was to determine our spiritual direction, the attitude that we could stick with throughout the coming ordeal. We chose to be positive, and to open ourselves to the support of others, no matter what form it took. We found reasons why we believed Emily's recovery was imminent and dwelled on them as if each was its own mantra.

Over the weekend, Mother's Day, the story goes, we lamented that we had to wait until Monday to see a surgeon, but in retrospect the wait was good. It gave us time to do the necessary self-reflection and meditating that was needed to give strength to our chosen direction. And it gave us time to start putting out the positive energy that we needed to multiply faster than Emily's cancer cells. Writing my first letter last Tuesday was one way we did that. Your calls and letters and prayers were part of that multiplication process and the four of us thank you for your love and support. We felt it.

In my letter, I told you that on Monday we realized breast cancer surgery was inevitable. We told the surgeons we wanted the surgery as soon as possible. We figured we would go in early the next week at best. On Tuesday, Emily took a sick day from work and just rested, which meant running errands and performing tasks for the house (like paying the bills) that she usually does at night after work. On Wednesday, she returned to work.

But midway through the day, I got the call at home that the operating team could perform together on Friday. I called Emily, who spent the rest of the day tying up loose ends to hold her job until she returns in six weeks.

On Thursday we didn't have a lot of time to think, or to dwell on the unknown, because we had so many appointments: with an acupuncturist, a nutritional oncologist, our rabbi and chazzan, the plastic surgeon's office, and Emily's massage therapist. Mom and Dad were coming up anyhow because Carrie was playing the lead female role in two performances of HMS Pinafore at her school, also on Friday. On Thursday evening, we watched a video performance of Wednesday's dress rehearsal because Emily would be under the knife the next day while Carrie was on stage.

The next morning, we checked in at the hospital at 6:15. Prep for the surgery began at 7:30 and the initial incision was made, according to hospital records, at 8:48. By noon, the mastectomy stage of the surgery was done. The surgeon came out to tell the folks and me that it had gone fine. We left the hospital then for lunch and to see Carrie's first performance.

I returned to the hospital after the play and stayed until 5:30. When word came down to the waiting room that the reconstructive phase was going fine and would probably be over in three hours, I left for Carrie's second performance, from 7-8. I returned immediately after. The surgery was actually completed at 9:20. The plastic surgeon reported to me that all had gone well.

I was able to see Emily in the recovery room and spend Friday and Saturday nights with her. They kept her drugged up all day Saturday and most of Sunday, their mission being to suppress the pain.

But by Monday they were working toward reducing amounts and/or having Emily take her meds orally instead of intravenously, and Emily was stretching the intervals between doses. On Sunday she began eating real food though getting a vegetarian-friendly menu was a surprising challenge. Sunday she sat up in her chair for a three-hour stretch. Monday she took a few walks around the hospital floor.

And yesterday she came home to begin a new phase. It will be slow. You look for laughs whenever you can. I had great fun yesterday, you can be sure, when I spent FIVE hours trying to get her prescription filled. Meijers didn't stock one of the three items, the prescribed pain killer, and neither did the first eight pharmacies they called for me. When I finally found one that did, the pharmacist discovered that the surgeon who wrote the prescription had written it for a strength that doesn't exist so I had to get a new prescription.

Meanwhile, the two items Meijers did sell me were wrong so I have to go back to return them. It's a small tsouris [Yiddish for pain in the butt] compared to how wonderful it is to have Emily back home.

Love,
Ken

Thursday May 25, 2000

Just wanted to get out the word that Emily's lymph nodes contained no cancer cells so she is clear.

Phew!

Love,
Ken

Sunday June 11, 2000

I wasn't planning on sending regular Emily announcements but I've had a few requests for an update. All I'm doing at this time is scribbling down notes in my journal so that's all I have to share.

Overall, though, we're doing fine. I say that knowing that you understand that everything is relative. We have cancer in our family now. Emily and I practiced saying the word that first Friday before Mother's Day when we learned the news. We didn't hide it in euphemisms or say "the c word." So, relative to the fact that we're dealing with cancer, we're doing fine.

Every time we've had to make a decision, I believe we've made the right one, especially sharing the experience and our feelings with David, Carrie, and all our friends and relatives. The calls and visits and flowers and emails and other acts of love that we've received have been a blessing and if I didn't thank you personally please accept my appreciation and Emily's here. You've been a source of strength.

Emily has never been good at seeing how loved she is. She's having a hard time blocking it now — a bright spot in the darkness. With the news that her lymph nodes were clear, we declared that we had won. Although we're not crazy about the chemo, we're relating to it as the cleanup operation whose negative effects will be minimized by all the positive moves we're making.

Here are my notes.

Love,
Ken

Friday June 2, 2000

Third acupuncture treatment today, first time on Emily's chest and stomach instead of back. Emily says she feels something. Was feeling heat in her breasts this morning. Charles Lincoln, our acupuncturist, says her body and mind still are in denial about the shock they underwent. Made next appointment for week from today.

Emily spoke on the phone for over an hour yesterday with Lenore Bernstein, from Temple Beth Emeth, another survivor, who spoke at the healing service at TBE last Friday. She said the third day after each chemo treatment is the worst. Emily got the call yesterday from the hospital that she will be beginning her chemo treatments on Monday June 12 so we made our next appointment for Thursday June 15.

Lenore also said the chemo is extremely cold going in but that Emily can request that they cut back the pressure. She urged us to request a tour of the facilities. She offered to loan Emily her wigs, which she no longer needs—she had no idea a wig isn't a wig if you want insurance to cover it. It's a "cranial prosthesis."

The actual chemo ritual takes two hours, though I don't know what's involved yet besides take dose and wait. Is it injected intravenously or taken like cough medicine? Is it being injected the whole two hours or is most of our time there spent waiting for it to take effect? Also, what I want to know most, with there having been no cancer in the lymph nodes and with all the specialists so far agreeing that Emily is healing much better than most, can they cut back on the strength or duration of the dose, and will they modify the dose and duration in the coming weeks according to Emily's progress? If they will, how do they measure progress, and how will the chemo affect Emily's recovery from her surgery?

The hospital has us scheduled to get chemo the same day we go in to learn about what's happening—in fact, an hour later. We need time to process, so Emily's going to call the hospital today to talk to someone.

On the way back from the acupuncturist, we stopped by the Temple to meditate in the chapel. Slow breaths, alternating between deep and shallow, feeling the air in the head, the neck, the shoulder, hands, and fingers, the chest and stomach, the lower body down to the toes, chanting Shalom but not sure if I should chant both syllables on the inhale and again on the exhale or one on each step, settling on both for in, both for out, then spacing out and not saying it at all; thoughts float in and out of my mind, and I fight them because I think I'm not supposed to be having thoughts; then I give in to them and they disappear into total absence of thought, and then another thought comes and goes in the same way. My body seems to float and then I leave my body, returning only to cough after too deep a breath or to scratch an irritating itch that stays behind even as my thoughts come and go.

Emily said she saw her father, who was dying of cancer right around the time Emily and I were first meeting 23 years ago and who David is named after. He and a group of angels were together in Emily's vision. Then they disappeared but one stayed behind and supported Emily by lightly holding her shoulders.

Sunday June 4, 2000

Went to Cancer Survivors' Day at Washtenaw Community College, sponsored by University of Michigan Hospital Cancer Center, where Emily had her surgery. Booths displayed information on physical therapy, Gilda's Club (after Gilda Radner), diet and nutrition, facial makeup, and other bits of information dedicated to the theme of surviving. An emcee was teaching anyone who wanted how to swing dance. It was uplifting to see women sporting buttons saying they were survivors of [fill in the blank]: 7 years, 20 years, 40 years!

One woman was a 22-year survivor who had had surgery at age 70. Do the math. She was looking forward to a trip to Alaska. Emily, who was the new kid on the block, being a survivor of 3 weeks (she listed, as did some others, from the time the cancer was discovered), amazed others who met her with how great she looked. That's what everyone's saying: the surgeons, survivors. We, of course, have no basis on which to judge but it helps to hear that anyway. She wasn't quite standing upright and she still relied on me for support but every day is an improvement, and we're doing a lot of laughing.

Monday June 5, 2000

Emily goes for her checkup with the plastic surgeon. He's thrilled with his handiwork. Emily is, too, with her perky boobs of a 20-year-old. Fifty years from now, when her friends' boobs are all sagging, she says, she'll still be walking upright.

Speaking of upright, the surgeon is pleased with Emily's progress at standing up straight and says that she can be standing straighter. Emily was concerned that stretching her insides to stand upright might cause damage but he said that stretching is exactly what she should be doing so that as she continues to heal she will be achieving higher states of limberness.

Emily isn't as good with lifting her left arm so the surgeon gave us a referral to begin visiting the physical therapist who happens to work in the shopping center nearly where we live. She'll start there in about two weeks.

Wednesday June 7, 2000

Emily has MUGA scan to test strength of heart before chemo begins next week. Will have another at end of chemo. Technician could only get one picture because Emily still can't lie down flat—she's only been walking upright for the past two days and it's still a strain; and the camera is on a rotor that is set to be positioned at various angles over a horizontal body. But the technician said that picture was the most important one because it shows what percentage of blood the left ventricle is pumping. Other pictures, which she couldn't get, give overview of heart. We'll find out the results Monday when we go in for chemo.

Tante [Emily's Tante (Aunt) Bernice, David's godmother] flies in tonight for a ten-day visit; I pick her up at the airport. She gives me a nice squeeze with her hug and notes that she's doing that because she knows Emily can't hug tightly now. I felt sad when I heard that; I had put it out of my mind. Her hug felt good; I lingered and we held hands as we walked through the airport.

I'm amazed at the outpouring of help we've received. Gloria [Emily's mom] just left Sunday after being here a week. The day Tante leaves, Janna [Emily's brother's daughter] arrives for a week, to be followed by Sue [Janna's mother] and Lorraine [Emily's oldest friend from New York; Carrie's godmother]. The folks come up every time no one else is here. They'll be coming up next week for a day so they can see Tante. Emily's brother and his [second] family will be visiting in the middle of July.

When friends offered to help, I didn't know what to tell them to do. But when Martha and Mary brought meals last week, or when Kathie washed Emily's hair and Lorraine [different Lorraine] gave her a hand shower before she was able to wash herself, I was able to spend those extra hours working on the computer catching up from the work time I've lost since Mother's Day weekend. Monday, Bev brought a Middle Eastern spread of tabouli, hummus, baba gannoujj, rice, pita bread, peppers, and salad. Tuesday, Judith brought pasta and salad. Today I ate leftovers all day.

Thursday June 8, 2000

Jon, Elissa, Jenny, and four beautiful first cousins once removed visit. The kids are life affirming to Emily and give her strength, a hint to any cousins with small kids who might be thinking of cancelling a visit because they don't want to get in our way.
Emily isn't taking pain killers anymore during the day, by the way, only at night, and even those she's spreading farther apart.

Friday June 9, 2000

Sixteen needles today at the acupuncturist, including four in feet and legs and 12 in stomach and chest. Emily feels water dripping out of her arms. Charles says it's only blood flow changing. In the old days, the Chinese inserted small bamboo pieces into the skin, then rotated them back and forth to create the necessary action in the body.

Today, small pins are flicked into the skin. Then a few of them—four today—are connected via wires to an electrical machine that transmits surges through the body for 20 minutes. Afterwards, Charles' assistant, who is from China and is still struggling with English, takes out the pins and dabs a disinfectant called Wah-tor that is a Chinese herbal remedy. "So you want us to think that's a remedy but it's really only water," I say to him. He doesn't get it and I don't push it but Emily laughs.

In the waiting room, we talk with one of the family doctors who work at that medical center. He says he's doing a cluster study of 40- to 50-year old women in Ann Arbor with breast cancer because it's like a plague.

Emily goes through periodic depressions—yesterday was a bad day. She spoke today with the nurse of the surgeon who will be administering the chemo. She said it was okay for Emily to take Xanax, a relaxant drug, the night before the chemo. "In fact, you can take it just before you come in." Emily was relieved.

Me? Picture a combination of denial, hyperactivity, and absolutely going with the flow mixed with loneliness and tendency to flip out if too many little things go wrong at once. Besides that I've reached a higher level of productivity; I just finished writing a book last week.

The kids have both talked to their friends about their mom's cancer. I'm sure they don't belabor it, as hopefully they don't feel a need to do, but Emily and I both are pleased that they haven't tried to hide it. Carrie's teachers say she's doing great. When Emily asked how he was feeling, David said fine; when pressed, he admitted he had some concerns but that overall he was confident.

Before cancer, Emily was a walker. Her routine included a brisk 20- to 40-minute walk every night during nice weather and a comparable stint on the treadmill in bad weather. Yesterday, Emily walked all the way around our block for the first time, a post-cancer record. The treadmill is strictly off limits for now.

Thursday June 15, 2000

Love, Kindness, Strength, and Joy

Emily bought her cranial prosthesis Monday. The event followed a series of mundane events: get kids off to school, pick up mail at post office, go out to Big Boy for morning decaf, photocopy form for Carrie's music camp, go to bank.

At the cranial prosthesis shop, the designated fitter, who helped Emily model CPs last week, noted that Emily must be feeling better. "You don't have your little pillow [that Emily held against her stomach at all times when she came home from the hospital]."

She informed Emily that the model she had ordered was in but since she didn't know what exact color Emily wanted she had ordered it in two colors, blond with white layers and blond with golden layers. The white-layered one made Emily look older. Guess which one she took. The CP was short-haired in the style Keith, our hairdresser friend, had cut Emily's own hair last week in anticipation of Emily's losing her hair from the chemo. "It's a little too long but Keith can play with it," Emily determined. It has "a nice neckline" and it "fits like a swim cap."

On the way home, we stopped to meditate at the chapel in the temple, Tante, Emily, and me. In my chair, I slouched, I sat straight, I sat with hands clasped on my lap trying to find a comfortable position to hold for 20 minutes. I sat with my hands hanging to the side and with my hands resting one on each lap and all the while I meditated, sometimes aware of my squirming, at others not. While I was meditating, I saw the Joy in this greater occasion and concluded, without understanding exactly why, that my vision was logical. When I told Emily what I had seen, she said she had seen three words: Love, Kindness, and Strength. I asked her to add Joy, and then to consider with me those four words as our mantra.

The night before, as Emily sat in her reclining chair in front of the TV, she had lamented that her body had failed her. In meditation, it occurred to me that her body hadn't failed her at all. In fact, it had held out exactly long enough for her to get herself situated in the best life position she's ever enjoyed, and that awaits her after her recovery period is ended. But it took a beating getting her there. "Now you have to reward your body by giving it the medicine and nutrients it needs to heal." Chemo is a less pleasant part of that process.

Staying on the Main Line of Life

After a quick lunch, Tante, Emily, and I went to the University of Michigan Cancer Center for our first chemo treatment. Tante, a 7 1/2-year survivor herself, came as the voice of experience. She was nonchalant on the outside and laughed as Emily shared stories of what had happened to others on chemo and assured Emily that every situation is different.

Your Partner Has Breast Cancer

Because the post-surgery tests showed Emily's lymph nodes to be clear, the attitude of the surgeons and their teams is that we most likely have won the battle against cancer. But because cancer cells can and sometimes do bypass the lymph nodes to enter the bloodstream, there is the possibility that some cancer is still in the body. For this reason, some amount of chemo follows almost every operation.

When we had first met with Sofia, our chemo surgeon, the day after Mother's Day, she had hinted that, because of what she knew so far from Emily's various tests up to that time, we could anticipate eight treatments. Now, as Emily tensed up for her first treatment, Sofia, who personally drew up Emily's treatment plan, reported that, because Emily's test results were good and she's healing quickly, we'd only have to come in three more times. Sessions are three weeks apart, which means we'll be done by the middle of August (but then go on Tamoxifen for the next five years).

Sofia's pre-chemo last-minute pearls of profundity as she handed me the prescription for the drugs Emily will take at home between treatments: "Do not accept the theory that the world is divided between pukers and non-pukers"—but take the meds as prescribed whether you think you need them or not.

Emily's positive assessment is due to her otherwise excellent health and health habits. Nurse Ginny encouraged her to keep them up during and after her treatments. "Sixty percent of women work, maintain energy, walk. Don't think of yourself as a sick person. This is not a culture of sickness; it's a culture of wellness. The cancer is just a sideline. Try to stay on the main line of life."

Tante added her take: "I have cancer; cancer does not have me."

Nice Place to Hang Out

Actually, it turns out the clinic is a pretty nice place to hang out as long as you've got to be there anyhow. The medical assistant gave us a tour as she led us to the treatment area. On the right side of the hallway leading to the treatment area was a kitchen where patients and their guests can find bagels, cream cheese, jelly, a toaster, coffee, decaf, soda, and popsicles (but not to take home with them, we were warned). Across the hall a few steps ahead was the pharmacy where they mix the chemo. And then we came to the chemo treatment area: 15 reclining seats, no waiting, 7 overhead TVs, 2 guest chairs per patient.

As the nurses set up the intravenous equipment and connected it to a vein on Emily's right side (where she still had lymph nodes), they gave us an overview of what to expect. The saline solution rinse treatment began at 5:10. This treatment would continue the whole while Emily was hooked up.

As I may have written earlier, about Emily's hospital stay, the mantra at UM Cancer Center is "Control pain and nausea," or "Any pain is too much pain." By the time any chemo entered Emily's body, she was already on three anti-nausea drugs and an anti-anxiety drug. The anti-nausea drugs—Kytril, Dexadine, and Tourcan—were either taken as pills or infused. When I asked the nurse how many milligrams were in two Kytril pills, she said, "about $100 worth." At 5:20, the Ativan drip began coming in through the same tube as the saline solution. "You won't be feeling sick today," the nurse said. For the next 15 minutes, Emily came in and out of dozing, but by 5:35, when the Ativan tube squeezed its last drop into Emily's vein, she was feeling high.

A minute later, the nurse was ready to administer the first of the two chemo drugs. Emily called for a timeout and said the Shema. For the next 16 minutes, two syringes of Adriamycin invaded Emily's bloodstream, followed by 50 minutes of Cytoxin. We were relieved to already be a quarter of the way done with our chemo adventure.

During her treatment, Emily felt pressure and agreed the fluid felt cool, but it was nowhere nearly as cold as Lenore, our survivor friend, had predicted. Tante laughed at one more preconception Emily had carried with her because of anecdotal information that turned out to be only specific to the storyteller.

Because the first four days after each treatment are considered the worst, Sofia earlier had written prescriptions for the four anti-nausea/anti-anxiety drugs, all in pill form, to take at home, each according to specific instructions and only on those 16 days. I had taken them to be filled at the general pharmacy on our way to the clinic. On our way out, I picked them up. One of them cost $1,230!

Because we have good insurance, we only paid $20 for that one, but can you imagine what house we'd be living in if we didn't have that insurance? (Other itemized costs associated with Emily's mammogram and her hospital stay approach $27,000.)

The Next Three Days

Tuesday, Emily only got sick once but she insists chemo wasn't the culprit. "I got something stuck in my throat." She was tired much of that day and the next but she's walking more.

Today, being the third day after chemo, she expected it to be her worst, as Lenore had predicted. It wasn't. In fact, Emily looked like she wasn't bothered by anything. (I know she had her discomfort; she just didn't show it.) At acupuncture, she laid down for the first time. All 14 needles were poked into her stomach and chest area, and toward the end of her 20 minutes a sudden release of energy on her painful right side flashed from her chest down to her toes.

In the afternoon I took her to her appointment with James, our nutritional oncologist. By the time the session was done, late afternoon, I was feeling uptight, restless, and angry. I attributed my feelings partly to the fact that medical appointments sandwiched around a shopping excursion had stolen my morning writing time and left me little other work time thereafter; and partly to my skepticism concerning the value of this particular leg of our strategic recovery plan, based largely on a cost-to-value assessment.

But as I was driving to Big Boy Restaurant, where I do a lot of my writing, it occurred to me that, as Emily's partner in recovery, I had driven to this session with an open mind, and I hadn't been angry until James told Tante and me to wait in the waiting room while he talked to Emily alone. When I returned home from Big Boy, I told Emily I would open up my mind again but only if it was understood that I was a participant in every session. Emily said she didn't want it any other way.

Friday June 16, 2000

I went to David's school this morning to pick him up after a short final day. While I was waiting for him in front of the school, a friend whose children go to the same school, and whose car was parked in front of mine, left the school and headed toward her car. When she saw me sitting in my car, she came over to say hello.

She asked me how I was doing. I said I was fine, like I always say as my transition sentence into a more detailed answer. And then I started giving her a more detailed answer.

I told her that Emily had just had a bilateral mastectomy followed by complete reconstructive surgery; that she was home now recuperating; and that she had just had her first of four chemo treatments and was doing fine. And then I explained that Emily had made the decision to go for the bilateral because for some reason the cancer cells had not all shown up in the various tests they had done on the cancerous left breast, which suggested the possibility that, even though it had tested clean, the right breast might be harboring invisible cancer cells as well.

Suddenly my friend pushed back from the car and threw up her hands. "Stop!" she shouted, and at first I thought she was just showing empathy with my own situation. But I was wrong.

"I just had a lumpectomy ten days ago," she continued. "They did radiation, I thought I was clean, and now for some reason they want me to come in again for more tests."

There's a plague out there.

I told Emily this story when I got home. She called our friend to offer support.

Monday June 19, 2000

Our friend, Susie, calls Emily to say that she has to have a mastectomy. She hasn't decided yet about a bilateral or reconstructive surgery.

Tuesday July 25, 2000

Hello, All,

Thanks to so many of you for your kind words. We're hanging in here. The worst is over.

Emily had her third chemo treatment yesterday so we only have one more to go. The trips are becoming routine. Get there on time. Wait incessantly because the doctors don't think anyone else has anything else to do that day. Get zapped. Leave.

We got to the hospital for our 10:30 blood test but the surgeon who was supposed to see us afterwards at 11 didn't actually see us until about 1, so by the time we got to the chemo part of the day we were late for that appointment and had to wait another 45 minutes. We finally got in at 2:30; we were out just before 5. I always bring work with me and try to pretend I'll be able to accomplish something but I usually don't. Yesterday was no exception.

Meanwhile, Emily chatters with the nurses, all of whom she knows, and the patients, who either she recognizes from previous sessions—or she doesn't. It doesn't really matter to her, especially once the drugs kick in. "Hi, what's your name? Where are you from? What are you in for?" Kind of like being in jail. Or, if you can't relate to that analogy, substitute "What's your major" for "What are you in for?" and you're at your first college dance.

Yesterday she sat next to an older man on one side of her who's been coming in every week and is almost done (she sat next to him during the last treatment three weeks ago) and a young woman who just recently started coming in, for I think uterine cancer, and has no idea how long she'll have to continue coming. Compared to both of them, we've been lucky; we knew what we had, we had a definite duration, four treatments, we're almost done, and we have a completely positive prognosis awaiting us. The woman sitting to Emily's right had a full head of hair but I imagined it was really a wig, although I couldn't really tell.

Emily still has some hair, though it's extremely thin. It's been falling out for about three weeks but it's only been noticeable the last two weeks. She started to cry recently while we were taking a walk when someone looked at her and she was convinced he thought she was hideous.

To me she still looks beautiful but I would be self-conscious, too, if it was me whose hair was falling out (actually mine is falling out but that's a different story). I told her that he was probably admiring how brave she was or some such stupid comment that was exactly the wrong reply to make at that time.

She rebuked my effort to make her feel better and let me know that she was strong 90% of the time but that sometimes she had to feel the sadness. I let her feel her sadness then and didn't say anything else until she asked me to continue what I had been saying before the interruption.

Since that experience, she's been wearing a babushka when we go out—she looks like a Russian peasant so it's kind of a back-to-the-roots thing. When we go out to restaurants, she'll wear her wig (insurance has already covered it; I don't have to call it a cranial prosthesis anymore).

She's been going to an acupuncturist every week, a nutritional oncologist every two or three weeks, and her massage therapist at least once a month, and all agree she's doing great; plus a monthly support group for cancer survivors at the University of Michigan Cancer Center. She's off all dairy and sugar, we're already vegetarians and eat organically at home, she's megadosing green tea tablets, taking regular doses of Vitamin E, staying off extra Vitamin C (because cancer cells seem to thrive on it) and multi-vitamins, ingesting a prescribed dose of Immunocal, an awful powder that tastes like sawdust but is actually a precursor to glutathione, which is supposed to protect the good cells, especially around the heart, as the chemo attacks the bad cells, and we're meditating regularly and learning about the Kabbalah (reading *God Is a Verb*, by David A. Cooper). Emily's walk time is back to her usual 20 minutes and her pace is almost back to normal, and her physical therapist is helping Emily get her muscles strong and limber. As I write she's lying on the floor bench pressing cans of beans.

Oy, and I'm trying to keep up with work between schlepping her to doctors. But she's been driving again for the past two weeks so she's regaining her sense of independence. As of this writing, she is planning to return to work on Thursday August 24. Four or five weeks later, she will be flying to Mexico on a business trip.

From the Kabbalah we learn that every seven years is significant. We're on our 21st year of marriage. What does that say?

From *God Is a Verb:*

> It is said in the Zohar that "when God delights in a soul, God inflicts suffering on the body so that the soul may gain full freedom." And, in another place, "When suffering comes to a good person, it is because of God's love. The body is crushed to give more power to the soul, so that it will be drawn nearer to God in love."
>
> This teaching is difficult for us. It should be another way, we feel. Good things should happen to good people. But this clearly is not the mystical viewpoint. A soul has the task of mending itself and the world to raise everything to a higher level of consciousness. There are an infinite number of ways to do so. Sometimes an impaired physical body is precisely what is needed to raise consciousness. Sickness, a difficult environment, a troubled relationship, poverty, suffering, untimely death of a loved one, any of a wide variety of demanding human experiences can lead to higher awareness. Because "gaining higher awareness"

is another way to say "coming closer to God" or "fulfilling a primary purpose of creation," whatever we experience in these physical bodies that brings us to this goal is viewed as another opportunity to raise holy sparks.

Indeed, overcoming life's challenges does a great deal more to mold the character of a person than not being tested at all.

Obviously there are many trials we would rather not have. Yet this may be what is on our plate. We do not necessarily get to choose. The way we learn to handle what we are given as our portion will affect the development of the soul.

I think we've each jumped a level of consciousness in the past two months.

Love,
Ken

Monday July 31, 2000

News is slow on the cancer front. I find myself writing less when not much is happening and then thinking I should be writing everyday to keep current.

But good health makes less dramatic reading than tragedy. I'm grateful for the opportunity to write on a topic that will make less dramatic reading.

The follow-up days to Emily's third chemo treatment were the least stressful of the three. Although she precedes every walk with me by announcing, "I'm not moving real fast," in fact her pace is almost up to her pre-cancer average. She's back to cooking dinners. Today she'll drive Carrie to her 1 p.m. dentist appointment.

It's wonderful having her with me in the evening to mellow out together on the couch in front of a movie, falling asleep before it's halfway through, instead of her going to bed early and me staying up alone and falling asleep before it's halfway through.

During our walks, we share reflections from *God Is a Verb*. Last night, we talked about the Kabbalistic interpretation of "It all comes together." Years ago, when I was first re-exploring my long-rejected Jewish roots, at Temple Shaarey Zedek in East Lansing, an old Jew named Mr. Blackman, who used to drive in from St. John's with his wife to attend services, befriended me and taught me that Jews don't say bad things about people. I always remembered that lesson, have striven to follow that high standard, and have chided myself when I fell short. But I never read anything in a Jewish text that mentioned that principle.

Last night, I did. David Cooper talks often about raising holy sparks. On page 180, he writes that "the sages taught us that negativity separates us from humanity and God by psychologically covering our hearts with a thick membrane. We are strongly advised to avoid thinking negative thoughts or saying negative things about others. Rather, the idea is to cultivate positive states of mind, which we can accomplish in many ways: by spending quality time daily in contemplation, meditation, and prayer; by living skillfully so as to avoid causing harm directly or indirectly to any form of life; by being modest in our own needs, respectful of the needs of others, and satisfied with our station in life; and by letting go of pride and envy."

The kids, by the way, have grown and matured since our cancer adventure began. I don't write about them enough perhaps—I've been obsessed with Emily's cancer and my own response. But I notice them always. There's less arguing in the house. Oh, it's still there. David is just emerging from a difficult period. The teen years. Adolescence. Whatever. If there was a chance to harass Carrie he'd find it. If what we said made sense, he'd disagree anyhow. Porch light on at night. Door not double locked. Cassettes loose in the van. Dishes in the sink. Oy. Carrie, meanwhile, is just entering the period. Lights on. Dishes in sink....

But she's crying less and standing up more to David.

And David, as much as he'll hate to admit it, lets out his soft side more often.

Family dinners are still a special time together, as they always have been. But now, to Emily and me, at least, they're more profound. Yesterday afternoon we went together to Cousin Alex's birthday party and then to see Eddie Murphy's new movie, Meet the Klumps. After dinner together, we went our separate ways. Carrie's tearing through Harry Potter #4, David's just about through a multi-layered, complex Nintendo game (I still haven't beaten the original Mario game), I read *God Is a Verb*, Emily made phone calls. Later, when Emily and I were taking our walk, David went to a friend's. But before midnight he came back to spend the night, with a friend even, so we were all together again.

And now I'm at Big Boy, catching up. In the early weeks of Emily's recovery, I had to be available at intermittent times of the day, including mornings, which I usually—or, ideally—reserve for myself. With her driving again, I can resume, more often than not, my usual routine.

Big Boy manager Lori's daughter is in St. Joe's Hospital with a kidney problem. I wished her well and told her my wife was recovering from breast cancer surgery. Lori wished Emily well and asked how she was doing. I said fine and added, "In the early recovery days, all my energies were focused on Emily. Now I've got some free energy. I'll send it your daughter's way."

Wednesday August 16, 2000

Monday, Emily had her fourth and final chemotherapy treatment. My difficulty in writing about it now may be comparable to Emily's fear at that session. After the treatment, she admitted to feeling conflicting emotions. On one hand, she was relieved that she was done with chemotherapy, that she didn't have to submit her body to anymore lethal invasions. On the other hand, she was scared that if she let go the cancer would return.

On one hand, I'm relieved and grateful that this experience is almost over and that we have emerged victorious. On the other hand, I will miss the intensity of the experience and the closeness I felt with Emily during that time.

She now prepares to begin at least three years of taking Tamoxifen once a day. She isn't too worried about this phase. It's more tsouris than anything else. Our only question is whether or not to continue with Tamixifen after three years. Some studies have shown that after three years the good that Tamoxifen does actually reverses itself and it turns into a bad. James, our nutritional oncologist, doesn't know either way for sure but he pointed out a study that suggested that the effects reverse after three years. Ginny, the nurse to our chemo oncologist, noted 1-, 2-, and 5-10-year studies that weren't yet conclusive but leaned in the direction of no harm after three years.

We figure that by the time three years pass some conclusions will have been drawn and so we could decide then what to do next.

At the end of the chemo session, Nurse Lisa gave Emily a "Congratulations" diploma signed by all the nurses in that section. Of course, Emily cried.

Yesterday I got the diploma framed and presented it to her. She cried again.

Resources for Caregivers

CancerCare
www.cancercare.org
800-813-HOPE (4673)

Offers free support, information, financial assistance, and practical help to people with cancer and their loved ones. Includes valuable list of resources for support people including online telephone, and face-to-face support groups; workshops; publications; a question-answer section; and additional resources.

Cancer Support Community
www.cancersupportcommunity.org
888-793-WELL (9355)

Cancer Support Community is a national organization that provides support groups, stress reduction and cancer education workshops, nutrition guidance, exercise sessions, and social events. Its slogan is "So that no one faces cancer alone." Website includes helpful caregiver information on Who is a Caregiver?; Caregiver's Journey; and Tips for Caregivers.

Eiler, Larry
When the Woman You Love Has Breast Cancer.
Ann Arbor, MI: Queen Bee Publishing, 1994.
www.whenthewomanyoulove.com

Recounts the author's experience and lessons learned from his wife Sandy's battle with breast cancer. The author offers ways of dealing with the emotional strain throughout the process of diagnosis to recovery. Website includes list of breast cancer support organizations.

Empowering Caregivers
www.care-givers.com
info@care-givers.com

The organization was founded in October 1998 on AOL by Gail Mitchell, presumably to help herself in her own recovery, although the website doesn't answer that question. Two weeks later, they published their first newsletter online. In December, the site was launched. Besides offering their newsletter for free twice weekly, the site has recommended books, links to online and offline sources, a directory of alternative healing sources, humor, and more. The weekly chats are reason enough to log on if you don't have a confidante with whom you can share thoughts and ideas when your partner is unavailable.

Flierl, Peter
Prayer, Laughter & Broccoli: Being There When Your Wife Has Breast Cancer. Rev. ed. Los Angeles: Witty Fools Productions, 2012.
203-273-5168 or 877-733-0528
prayerlaughterandbroccoli.blogspot.com
wittyfools@aol.com

Your Partner Has Breast Cancer

Written as a result of the author's experience as a support person for his wife who discovered, at the age of 37, that she had stage 3 aggressive malignancy breast cancer. The author reflects on and shares his strength, faith, wisdom, courage, and common sense with other couples and families battling breast cancer together.

Loscalzo, Matthew J., and Marc Heyison
For the Women We Love - A Breast Cancer Action Plan and Caregiver's Guide for Men. Adamstown, MD: Men Against Breast Cancer, 2012.
www.menagainstbreastcancer.org

This is a no-nonsense navigation and survival guide for men who are committed to being there for the women they love. This book is a highly structured road map that will give you a better understanding of what the patient and caregiver are up against. This book will give men the right tools to make a real difference in the quality of survivorship of the patient and family.

Men Against Breast Cancer
PO Box 150
Adamstown, MD 21710-0150
866-547-MABC (6222)
www.menagainstbreastcancer.org
info@menagainstbreastcancer.org

Founded in 1999 by Marc Heyison, the first and only national 501 (c)(3) nonprofit organization designed to provide targeted support services that educate and empower men to be effective cancer caregivers. Website provides Find a Friend, an online resource for support people looking for other support people in their community to share thoughts and feelings; a collection of websites with useful breast cancer- and cancer-in-general-related information; non-web information sources about breast cancer; and video resources.

Silver, Mark
Breast Cancer Husband: How to Help Your Wife (and Yourself) through Diagnosis, Treatment and Beyond. Emmaus, PA: Rodale Books, 2004. https://www.rodalestore.com/breast-cancer-husband.html?___SID=U

    Silver addresses the role and the needs of husbands, fiancés, and boyfriends, with input from prominent healthcare professionals as well as over 100 couples who have fought breast cancer together. He acknowledges men's common feelings of panic and frustration as well as their natural instincts, which may lead them in the wrong direction in their attempts to "fix" the breast cancer. The book includes a glossary of medical terms, checklists of questions for doctors, information about breast reconstruction, tips on coping with the side effects and aftereffects of chemotherapy, and guidance for breaking the news to family members, especially the kids. Mostly, it helps husbands figure out what their wives need even as those needs change regularly.

When the Woman You Love Has Breast Cancer.
Chicago: Breast Cancer Network of Strength, 2008.
http://digital.turn-page.com/issue/2067

    This pamphlet contains information on the obstacles a couple that is dealing with breast cancer may face. Contents include initial doctor's visit and diagnosis, treatment options, surgery, coming home, follow-up treatment, the future, and staying committed. It discusses how to support your spouse or partner and gives information on feelings the support person may encounter through various stages of the experience along with how the relationship may be affected, including physical closeness and sexual intimacy. Available for free only on the Internet with an Adobe Acrobat Reader though the organization that publishes it, Breast Cancer Network of Strength, doesn't appear to be around anymore.

Final Word to Readers

Thank you for purchasing and reading *Your Partner Has Breast Cancer: 21 Ways to Keep Sane as a Support Person on Your Journey from Victim to Survivor*. If you found this book helpful, please be kind enough to review it on your blog, through your social media networks, or at your favorite retailer so that other caregivers can find it. Let's let no support person grieve alone. We're all in this together.

Your Partner Has Breast Cancer: 21 Ways to Keep Sane as a Support Person on Your Journey from Victim to Survivor is also available as an ebook through smashwords.com and amazon.com.

Coming soon in ebook and print: *Never Be Afraid: A Belgian Jew in the French Resistance*, the true story of Bernard Mednicki, a street-smart Belgian Jew from a working-class, Orthodox, socialist background, flees Belgium with his family in 1940 when the Nazis invade, assumes a Christian identity, and settles in Volvic, a small town in the mountainous region of southern France. There, a chance encounter with a prominent Nazi collaborator named Duhin forces Bernard to confess his Jewish roots and change the course of his destiny.

Other Books by Ken Wachsberger

Available in print from
www.voicesfromtheunderground.com:

Voices from the Underground Series (compiled and edited):

Insider Histories of the Vietnam Era Underground Press, Part 1

My Odyssey through the Underground Press (by Mica Kindman)

Insider Histories of the Vietnam Era Underground Press, Part 2

Stop the Presses! I Want to Get Off!: A Brief History of the Prisoners' Digest International (by Joseph W. Grant)

Available in print from www.azenphonypress.com:

Transforming Lives: A Socially Responsible Guide to the Magic of Writing and Researching

Beercans on the Side of the Road: The Story of Henry the Hitchhiker

The Ballad of Ken and Emily: or, Tales from the Counterculture

The Last Selection: A Child's Journey through the Holocaust (co-authors Goldie Szachter Kalib and Sylvan Kalib)

Facts On File Banned Books Series (edited)

About the Author

Ken Wachsberger, founder of Azenphony Press, is a long-time author, editor, educator, political organizer, and book consultant who has written, edited, and lectured widely on the Holocaust and Jewish resistance during World War II, the First Amendment, the Vietnam era, writing in the electronic age, copyright, teachers' rights, writers' rights, the I-Search paper, and writing for healing and self-discovery.

He did not set out to write about how to keep sane as a support person for a partner who has breast cancer but he had to do it to keep sane while he was a support person for a partner who had breast cancer. Fourteen years later, both Ken and his partner, Emily, are doing well.

Ken is also a book contract adviser with the National Writers Union as well as a former national officer, creator of the NWU's electronic Authors Network, and advocate of independent publishing.

For book offers, editing services, or speaking engagements, including booking a "Writing to Keep Sane" or 'Transforming Lives through Writing" workshop, he may be reached at info@azenphonypress.com.

Patient Education Resource Center

13482

Made in the USA
Middletown, DE
08 November 2015